FORCES Of NATURE

Volcanoes

TRACI STECKEL PEDERSEN

PERFECTION LEARNING®

Editorial Director: Susan C. Thies
Editor: Mary L. Bush
Design Director: Randy Messer
Book Design: Tobi Cunningham, Lori Gould
Cover Design: Michael A. Aspengren

A special thanks to the following for his scientific review of the book:
Jason Parkin, Meteorologist, KCCI Weather, Des Moines, Iowa

Image Credits:
©Royalty-Free CORBIS: p. 15; ©Roger Ressmeyer/CORBIS: p. 27; Associated Press: pp. 5, 10, 16, 18, 20, 21, 23, 24, 25

Photos.com: all background images, all cover images, pp. 14 (right), 29, 32; Istockphotos: pp. 3, 12, 14 (left), 19; Corel: p. 22; Perfection Learning Corporation: pp. 4, 6, 7, 8, 9, 11, 17

For information, contact
Perfection Learning® Corporation
1000 North Second Avenue, P.O. Box 500
Logan, Iowa 51546-0500.
Phone: 1-800-831-4190
Fax: 1-800-543-2745
perfectionlearning.com

PB ISBN-10: 0-7891-6606-2   ISBN-13: 978-0-7891-6606-7
RLB ISBN-10: 0-7569-4629-8   ISBN-13: 978-0-7569-4629-6

3 4 5 6 7 8 9 PP 19 18 17 16 15

Table of Contents

1
Chimneys, Sparks, and Angry Goddesses

In ancient times, one of the Aeolian Islands just north of Sicily made quite an impression on the people living in the area. They believed this fiery island was the chimney of Vulcan, the Roman god of fire. Vulcan was a blacksmith who would hammer out lightning bolts and weapons for other gods. As he did, clouds and chunks of "fire" would fly out of his chimney. The people named the island Vulcano.

Lava and clouds of ash erupt from the Merapi Volcano in Indonesia.

Volcanoes inspired many other myths and legends around the world. Each culture has its own version of how volcanoes came to be. One eruption was explained as the "sparks" flying between two warring gods. Another was the result of a goddess blowing her top in a fit of rage. The Hawaiian Islands were blamed on Pele, the goddess of volcanoes.

Volcanoes Today

Today there are still more than 500 **active** volcanoes in the world. They come in different shapes and sizes, have varying activity levels, and erupt in different styles. They blow out **lava**, ash, **cinders**, and gases. Many of them trigger mudslides, avalanches, earthquakes, and tsunamis. A volcano's destruction can be devastating.

Ancient cultures wove stories to explain volcanoes. Today we understand their science, but they are still a fascinating wonder of nature.

2 Beneath the Surface

We now know that volcanoes are not the result of the actions of gods. So then what *does* cause them? The answer begins beneath the surface of the Earth.

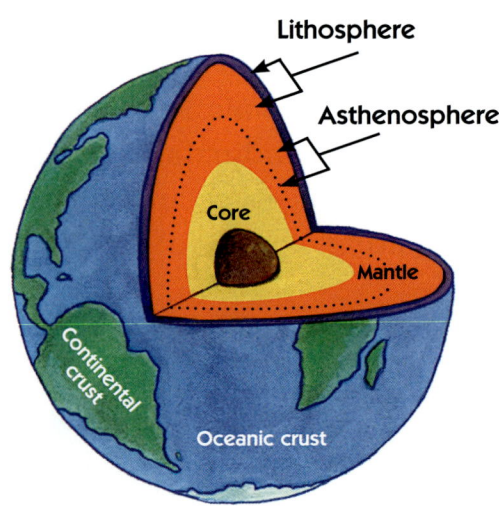

The Mantle

Under the Earth's crust is a layer called the **mantle**. The mantle is about 1800 miles thick. It is made of very hot rocks that cycle up and down in slow motion. Hotter areas of rock flow upward, cool, and sink down again in an endless cycle.

Tectonic Plates

The top part of the mantle and the Earth's crust form the lithosphere. The lithosphere is broken into more than a dozen different pieces called **tectonic plates**. The asthenosphere is just beneath the lithosphere. The asthenosphere is the remaining upper part of the mantle. The tectonic plates move slowly on top of the asthenosphere.

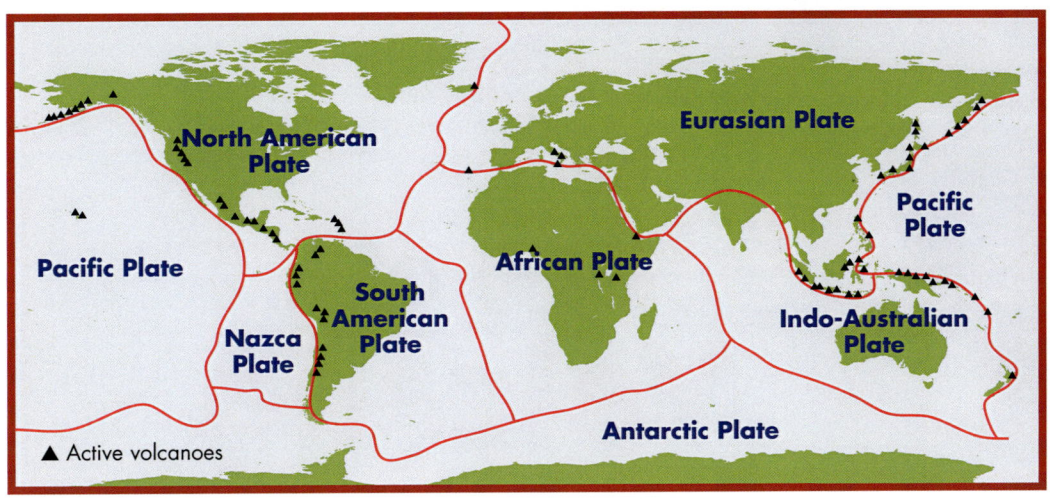

Earth's major tectonic plates

The movement of tectonic plates varies. Sometimes plates move apart. Other times they collide or scrape by one another. This interaction affects where and how volcanoes form.

Magma

Although the mantle is terribly hot, the rocks inside it generally remain solid because of the intense pressure. But when tectonic plates move or a crack appears in the crust, pressure is released. This allows rocks near the surface of the mantle to melt and become **magma**.

Magma is a mixture of liquid rock, solid rock, and gases. The materials that make up magma vary with location. But overall, oxygen and silicon are the most common elements found in magma. Water vapor, carbon dioxide, and sulfur dioxide are common gases present in magma.

Because magma is less dense than surrounding rock, it rises. Magma will continue to rise until something blocks its path. In many cases, this "block" is the Earth's crust. Here the magma collects under the surface, creating a magma chamber. A magma chamber is an underground space where magma collects. When the magma erupts onto land, it's called *lava*.

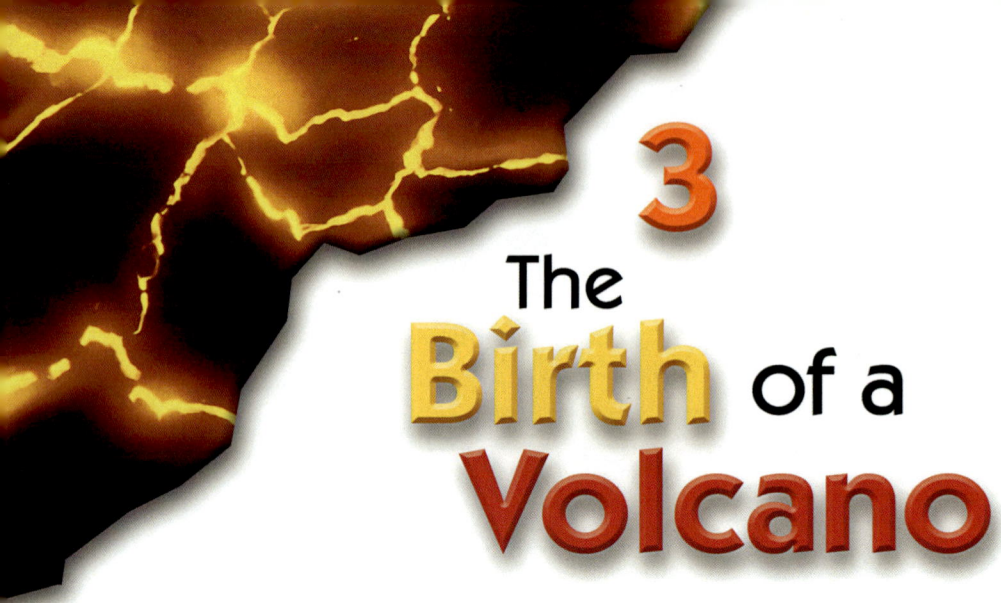

The Birth of a Volcano
3

The movement of the Earth's tectonic plates determines how volcanoes are formed. Most volcanoes take place near the edges of plates. A few, however, do occur far away from plate boundaries.

Subduction Zone Volcanism

Most volcanoes form when two plates collide and one plate slips below the other. This is called *subduction*. As the lower plate sinks into the mantle, a large **trench** is often formed.

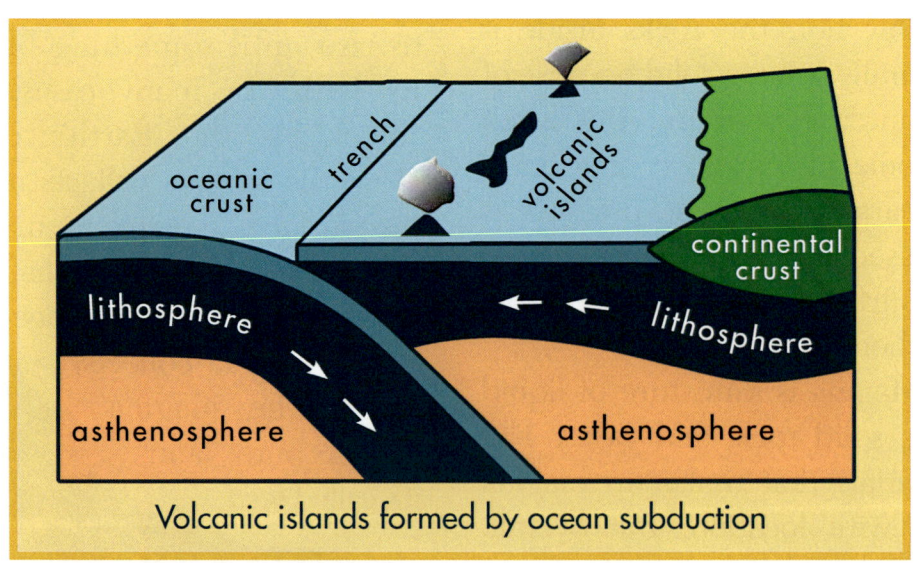

Volcanic islands formed by ocean subduction

The lower plate contains a large amount of surface water as well as water locked into its crust. As it's forced deeper into the mantle, extreme pressure and hot temperatures release the water from the crust. The water rises into the upper mantle. As the water seeps into the mantle, the boiling point of the rocks is lowered. This causes the rocks to melt into magma.

The magma is more buoyant than the surrounding rock, so it moves up through any available cracks and pores. When the magma emerges onto the surface of the Earth, it forms a chain of volcanoes along the trench.

When subduction happens under the ocean, a chain of volcanic islands is created. The Ring of Fire is a half-circle of volcanoes located in the Pacific Ocean. More than half of the world's active volcanoes are located in this ring.

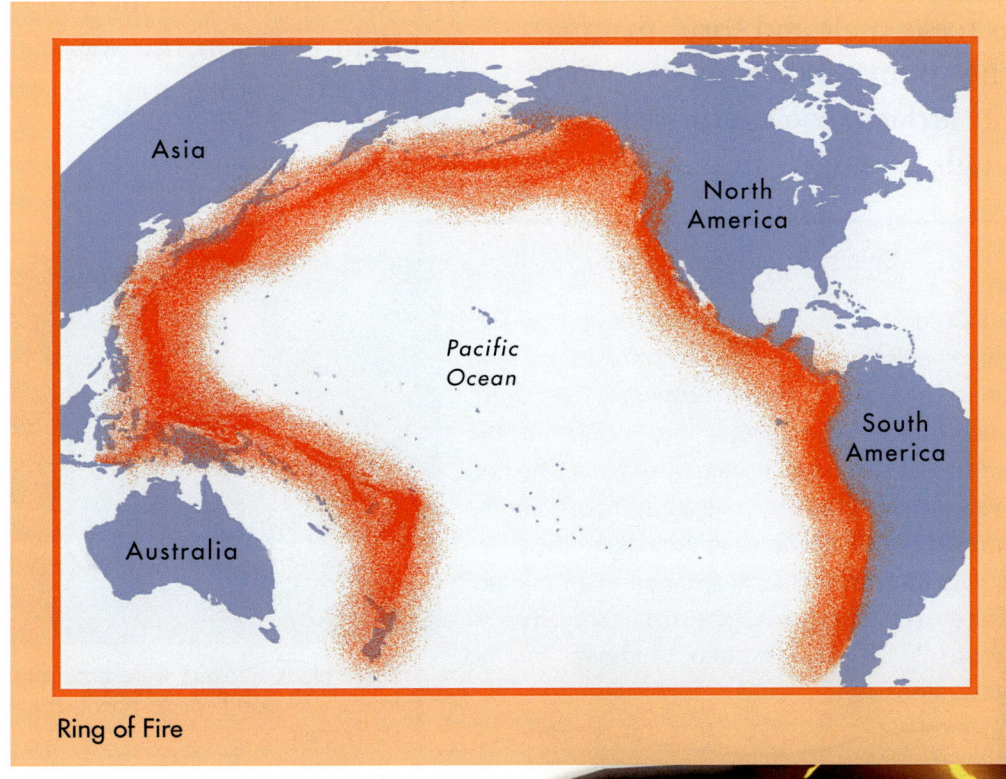

Ring of Fire

If subduction happens on land, it produces a chain of volcanic mountains. The Andes Mountains in South America and the Cascade Mountains in the United States are a result of subduction zone volcanism.

Spreading Center Volcanism

When two tectonic plates move apart, a gap opens in the lithosphere. Rocks from the mantle flow upward to fill in the crack. The pressure here is lower, so rocks melt and form magma. The buoyant magma reaches the surface, cools into rock, and builds a **ridge**. If the ridge is on land, it's called a *continental ridge*. Under the ocean, it's called an *ocean ridge*. This type of volcano formation is called *spreading center volcanism*.

Spreading center volcanism usually occurs under the ocean. As plates move apart, magma builds new seafloor crust. This is known as seafloor spreading.

The Mid-Atlantic Ridge in the Atlantic Ocean was formed from seafloor spreading. The Mid-Atlantic Ridge is the longest mountain chain in the world. It stretches for more than 10,000 miles.

Chimneys Under the Sea

Columns of black smoky water called *hydrothermal vents* or *black smokers* can be found in ocean ridge volcanoes. They form when ocean water seeps into cracks in the ocean's crust and gets heated by magma. The hot, metal-rich water is then driven upward in columns through cracks and holes in the ocean floor.

As the hot, smoky water comes in contact with the cool ocean water, the metals are released. Eventually they build up into "chimneys" on the ocean floor.

These black smokers were brought up from the ocean floor so scientists could study them.

Hot Spots

Volcanoes can also form in the middle of tectonic plates. Sometimes, unusually hot mantle material from the asthenosphere pushes its way into the upper mantle and melts into magma. The "pool" of magma takes the shape of a **plume** with a larger bottom and a long, narrow top. This hot plume of magma under the Earth's crust is called a **hot spot**.

A hot spot is a good place for volcanic activity. The hot spot stays still, but tectonic plates may pass over it. This can produce a chain of volcanic mountains or islands on the plate. Once the plate passes over the hot spot, the volcano becomes inactive, or **extinct**.

The Hawaiian Islands were formed by a hot spot that's estimated to be at least 70 million years old. Right now, the Big Island of Hawaii lies directly above the hot spot.

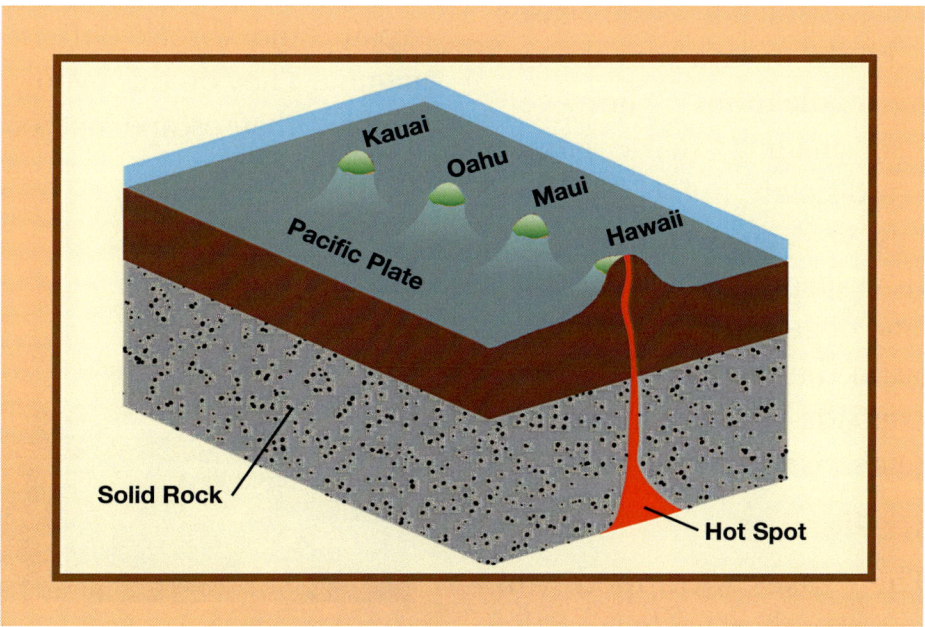

Kauai
Oahu
Maui
Hawaii
Pacific Plate
Solid Rock
Hot Spot

4 Make Way for the Magma

Have you ever shaken up a can of soda and then popped the top? What comes next is a blast of fizzy soda shooting into the air and on anything or anyone nearby. Some volcanoes erupt in a "shaken soda" sort of way, spraying toxic gases and chunks of lava into the air. Many volcanoes, however, release magma in a gentle flow—so slowly, in fact, that you can just walk away from it.

How magma moves out of a volcano depends on the quantity of gas in the magma, the inside and outside pressures, and the magma's **viscosity**.

Under Pressure

The gases "trapped" in magma stay there as long as the pressure from the surrounding rock is stronger than the **vapor pressure** exerted by the gas. A crack in the crust or cooling temperatures can decrease the outside pressure. When the vapor pressure inside is greater than the outside pressure, the gases expand and "break out" of the magma. They do this by forming bubbles that escape out of the melted rock.

Mount Vesuvius in Italy

The pressure and quantity of gas in an area of magma affect the force of the eruption. In general, higher pressure and larger amounts of gas result in bigger explosions.

Inquire and Investigate: Pressure and Eruptions

Question: How does pressure affect the force of a volcanic eruption?

Answer the question: I think that the higher the pressure, the _____.

Form a hypothesis: The higher the pressure, the (more/less) forceful the eruption is.

Test the hypothesis:

Materials
- 2 small, clear bottles of club soda
- sink or outdoor space

Procedure
Let the bottles of soda rest on a flat surface for several minutes. Then look closely at the soda. Are any gas bubbles visible while the soda is under the pressure of the closed bottle? Record your observations.

Without shaking it, open one of the bottles and look inside. Record your observations.

Now shake the second bottle vigorously. Then turn the bottle toward the sink or away from you outside and open it. Observe and record what happens.

Observations: No bubbles could be seen in either bottle at rest before the caps were opened. This is because the pressure in the bottle keeps the gas from expanding into bubbles. After opening the first bottle, gas bubbles could be seen jumping around. After opening the second bottle, the gas as well as the soda sprayed out violently.

Conclusions: The higher the pressure, the more forceful the eruption. In the first bottle, the pressure was released gently and the gas escaped slowly. This escape was marked by the bubbles that formed in the soda. In the second bottle, the gases were agitated, so there was more pressure in the bottle. When that pressure was released, the gas exploded out, taking the soda with it. The higher pressure caused a more forceful "eruption."

To Flow or Not to Flow

If you were to tilt a smooth surface and have a race between honey and water, which would win? The water, of course. This is because honey is more viscous than water. Viscosity is a thick, sticky consistency that gives a material the ability to resist flowing.

The viscosity of magma depends on the rocks that make it up. Basalt rock, for example, has low viscosity, while rhyolite has a high viscosity. So basaltic magma flows faster than rhyolite magma.

Lots of Lava!

The most violent eruptions typically come from magma with a lot of gas and high viscosity. This is because gas bubbles have a harder time breaking away from highly viscous magma. When they do finally escape, the magma shoots out with them. This causes a spectacular explosion of lava.

5
It's Going to Erupt!

Eruptions can vary from gentle flows to startling explosions. Some last only a day, while others continue for years. The type of eruption generally determines what shape a volcano will take as well.

Fissure Eruptions

Not all volcanoes have a conelike appearance like the ones usually shown in books and movies. Sometimes magma pours out of cracks, or fissures, in the Earth's surface. These fissures usually occur at plate boundaries.

In a fissure eruption, magma can flow out or spray upward a

short distance above the ground. This creates a "curtain of fire."

Fissure eruptions are one of the least violent types of eruptions. The lava flow is usually heavy and slow moving. Fissure eruptions can be found along ocean ridges as well as in Hawaii.

Hawaiian Eruptions

Hawaiian eruptions were named after the most common type of eruptions that take place in Hawaii. The magma in these mild eruptions has low viscosity and is low in gas content. The lava flows steadily from a central **vent**. If there are repeated eruptions and the lava spreads out over a wide area, a **shield volcano** may form. These are gently sloping volcanoes that usually cover a large area.

In some Hawaiian eruptions, a fountain of glowing orange lava shoots hundreds of feet into the air. These beautiful eruptions can last from just a few minutes up to several hours.

Mount Kilauea in Hawaii is a shield volcano.

Strombolian Eruptions

Strombolian eruptions are named after the volcano on the Aeolian Island of Stromboli. The lava in a typical Strombolian eruption is more viscous than Hawaiian lava. Gas pressure must be fairly high for an eruption to take place. During an eruption, small amounts of lava are pumped into the air in rhythmic bursts. Loud booms often accompany the eruption.

After a Strombolian eruption, ashy bits of volcanic rock and lava called **tephra** accumulate near the central vent. This forms a small **cinder cone volcano**. These volcanoes often have steep slopes and wide **summit craters**. The Izalco Volcano in Ecuador was created by a Strombolian eruption.

Vulcanian Eruptions

The Vulcano volcano lent its name to Vulcanian eruptions. The magma found in these eruptions has a high gas content and is highly viscous. This results in many short-lived but fairly big explosions. Large amounts of ash and **pyroclastic bombs** are thrown into the air. Pyroclastic bombs are large volcanic rocks that are ejected while still semimelted. The rocks are shaped as they cool and harden in the air. There is usually no lava flow in Vulcanian eruptions. The Sakurajima Volcano in Japan has recently demonstrated Vulcanian behavior.

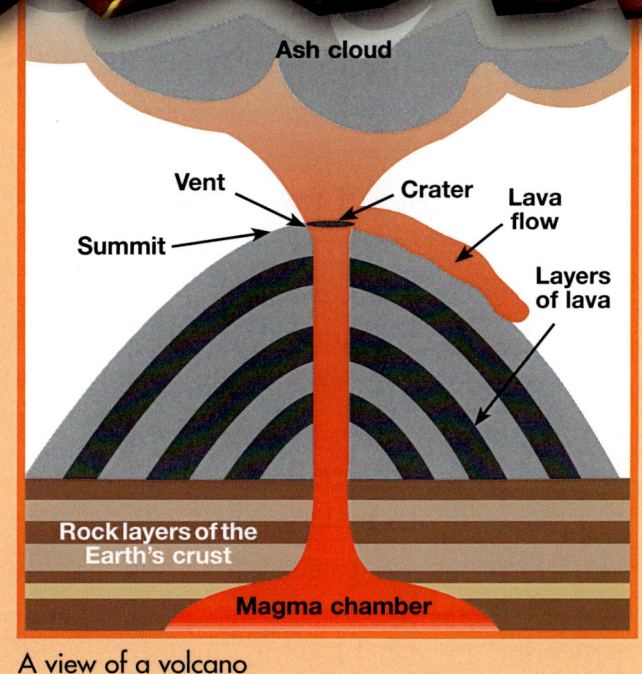

A view of a volcano

Plinian Eruptions

Because of their high gas content and viscosity, Plinian eruptions are some of the most violent on Earth. These explosive eruptions shoot up a towering plume of cinders and ash that can reach as high as 30 miles in the air. The explosion can last for many hours or even several days. Fast-moving lava can quickly overtake an entire area, devastating everything in its way.

Plinian eruptions often create **stratovolcanoes**. These are steep, cone-shaped volcanoes of ash, lava, and other volcanic materials. The tallest volcanic mountain on Earth, the Nevado Ojos del Salado in Chile, is a stratovolcano.

Pliny in Pompeii

The name *Plinian* comes from Pliny the Younger, a Roman soldier who witnessed a volcano destroy the city of Pompeii in 79 A.D.

Pelean Eruptions

Pelean eruptions are another type of violent eruption. These eruptions differ from Plinian eruptions because they shoot out glowing avalanches of fiery ash. The lava in these eruptions doesn't flow far, resulting in the formation of a **lava dome**. Lava domes are mounds of lava that accumulate near a volcano's vent. Often Pelean eruptions can be predicted because they are preceded by ash blowing out of the volcano.

Mount Pelée in Martinique is the first volcano where this type of eruption was recognized. That's where the name *Pelean* comes from.

Dead or Alive

Depending on their eruption history, volcanoes are labeled as active, **dormant**, or extinct. Although there is no exact agreement on these labels, active volcanoes are generally those that have recently erupted or are currently experiencing eruption activity. Dormant volcanoes are in a "sleeping" stage. They aren't experiencing current activity but show signs that they may do so in the future. Extinct volcanoes are those that haven't erupted in thousands of years and have almost no possibility of future eruption.

Magma oozes out of Mount St. Helens, forming a new lava dome.

6
Very
Famous
Volcanoes

The Earth is home to thousands of volcanoes. Certain ones, however, stand out because their eruptions were unexpected, devastating, or both. These are just a few of those famous eruptions.

Mount Vesuvius

In 79 A.D., the Plinian eruption of Mount Vesuvius completely destroyed the Italian cities of Pompeii and Herculaneum. About 10 feet of tephra fell on the city of Pompeii. The fishing village of Herculaneum was buried in about 75 feet of ash. More than 3000 people died.

Mount Vesuvius

The volcano erupted several times after 79 A.D., but the destruction wasn't nearly as great. Then the volcano remained quiet between 1300 and 1630. In 1631, another eruption took the local people by surprise. Lava and mudflows killed about 3500 people.

Mount Vesuvius last erupted in 1944. It is still considered an active, dangerous stratovolcano.

Mount St. Helens

Mount St. Helens is located in the Cascade Mountains in the state of Washington. The volcano had a history of eruptions, but until 1980, it had been quiet for 123 years. Then in the spring of 1980, the volcano showed signs of activity. Several earthquakes shook neighboring communities. Loud bursts of sound and steam came from the mountain. Snow on the mountainside became dark from escaping ash. The mountain bulged on its northern side as magma built up inside.

Finally, on May 18, the volcano erupted and the side of the mountain with the bulge collapsed. Debris from the huge landslide covered 24 square miles. Rock material was hurled as fast as 300 mph. A gigantic column of ash rose thousands of feet into the air and then drifted down. Thousands of acres of forests were wiped out, and 57 people lost their lives.

Mount St. Helens

Mount Kilauea

Mount Kilauea

Located above a hot spot, Mount Kilauea is the most active volcano on Earth. *Kilauea* means "spewing" or "much spreading." This is a perfect name for a shield volcano with constant lava flow. Much of this lava travels to the ocean coast.

Mount Kilauea's most recent eruption began in January of 1983. Its slow-moving lava, however, didn't begin to reach the ocean until November of 1986. In 1990, the flow from Kilauea buried two Hawaiian towns. The volcano is still erupting today.

Mount Pelée

Mount Pelée is located on the island of Martinique. It is part of an arc-shaped chain of islands that was formed by subduction. In early 1902, the people living on the island noticed that the stratovolcano was showing signs of distress. Explosions were heard coming from the volcano's summit. Tremors rocked the area. Ash showered down from the sky.

Citizens in the nearby city of Saint Pierre began to worry. However, no one on the island knew much about volcanoes, and it was decided that nothing serious would happen. After all, Mount Pelée's last eruption in 1851 had been mild, and no one had been hurt.

During Pelée's eruption, survivor Louis Aguste Cyparis was trapped in this jail cell. The thick walls protected him from the hot rock and gas.

But on May 8, Mount Pelée erupted in a rage. The beautiful, prosperous city of Saint Pierre was completely destroyed. Nearly 30,000 people died within seconds of breathing in the ash and burning fumes. Only two men survived the disaster.

One positive thing did come from the deadly eruption. When people around the world heard about the tragedy, they finally realized the importance of volcano prediction and preparation.

Scientist of Significance

Alfred Lacroix, a French geologist, spent a year studying Mount Pelée after the great eruption of 1902. The scientist discovered that an unusual phenomenon had occurred during the eruption. A glowing avalanche of hot, choking gas and rock had been produced by a sideward eruption of volcanic material. Lacroix called it *nuée ardente*, which means "fiery cloud." It was this hot ball of volcanic material that had raced down the mountain and destroyed the city of St. Pierre within minutes.

Lacroix wrote a book about his findings on Mount Pelée. The book made a significant contribution to volcanology, the study of volcanoes. Today scientists call the "fiery cloud" that Lacroix identified a *pyroclastic flow*.

7
Keeping an Eye on the Volcano

Volcanoes can sit for hundreds of years without any sign of eruption. So how can scientists know if one will erupt again, and if so, when? Today's volcanologists are equipped with the tools and technology needed to successfully predict most volcanic events.

A volcanologist keeps track of how often Mount Etna errupts. Mount Etna is a very active volcano in Italy.

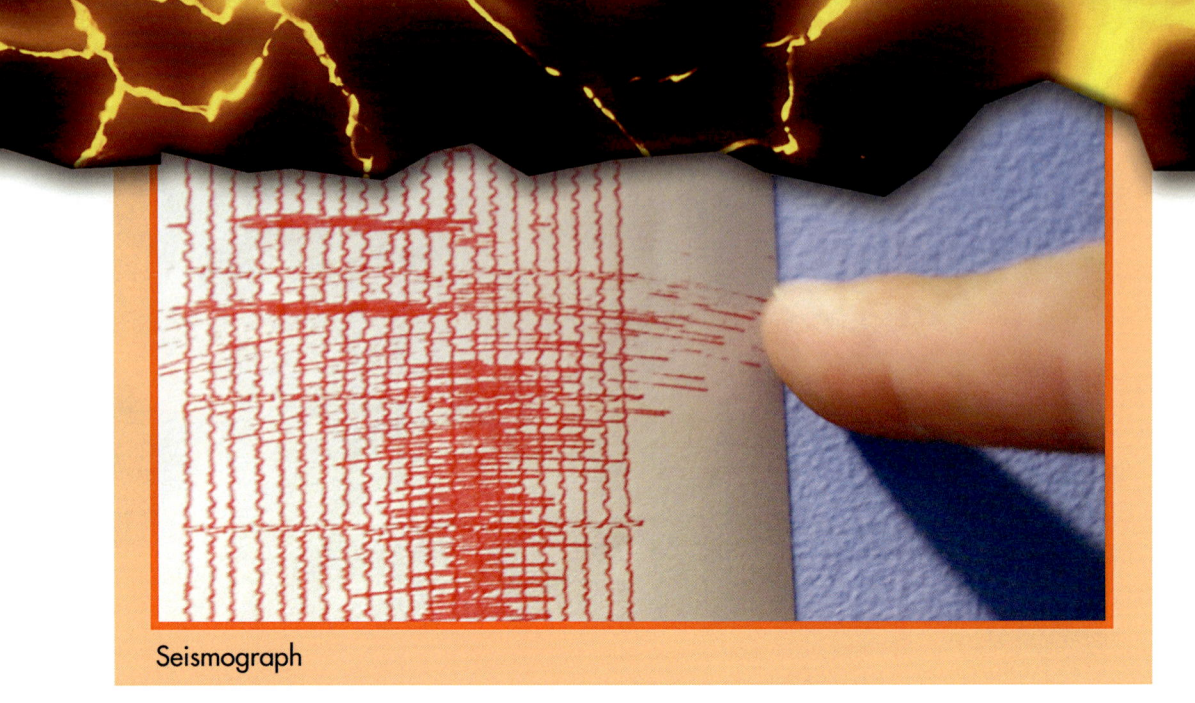

Seismograph

Reviewing the Past

A careful look into a volcano's past behavior is very important to the long-term prediction of future eruptions. Volcanologists carefully study the volcanic debris found on and around a volcano. The layers of hardened lava and other deposits left behind reveal a lot about the volcano's last eruption. The materials tell what type of eruption it was, approximately when it occurred, in which direction the blast was headed, and how forceful it was. This information can help predict future eruptions.

Seismography

Seismographs are used to "listen" to a volcano. A network of these instruments around a volcano can detect the earthquakes that come before a volcanic eruption. When magma moves, the Earth trembles. As the magma gets closer to the surface, the rumblings become stronger and occur closer together. These tremors are signs that an eruption will occur soon.

Ground Deformation Monitoring

Moving magma can deform, or change, the ground on or around a volcano. It can make a volcano's crust bulge outward, tilt to the side, or drop down. Several instruments can be used to detect and measure this **ground deformation**.

One way that scientists keep track of magma is by placing electronic tiltmeters on a volcano's surface. These instruments hold a small container filled with fluid. A bubble inside the fluid moves when a volcano's slope changes. Electrodes inside the bubble and fluid measure these changes.

Radar guns can be used to measure the speed of flowing lava.

An electronic distance meter (EDM) uses electromagnetic signals. Reflectors are set up on a volcano. A signal is sent from the EDM to the reflectors. The time that it takes for the signal to travel from the EDM to the reflectors and back is recorded. Changes in this time indicate ground deformation since it means the position of the reflectors has changed.

Global Positioning Systems (GPS) use **satellite** technology to monitor ground deformation. Satellites in outer space collect information from receivers on volcanoes. This data indicates any changes on or around a volcano.

A "Map" for Survival

Scientists use the information gathered from monitoring technology to create maps that highlight the areas of greatest danger around a volcano. People who live in these zones must be prepared for an eruption.

The flowing lava, poisonous fumes, and flying rocks of an erupting volcano can all be deadly. What can be done to protect against these dangers? The best precaution is evacuation.

Technology Link

The newest breakthrough in volcanology is radar interferometry. This is the use of satellites and radar technology to create pictures of ground deformation. These pictures are called *interferograms*. Interferograms combine images from satellites into one complete picture. The slightest ground movement can be shown in colorful, detailed diagrams.

Scientists are excited about radar interferometry because it shows the "whole picture" of ground deformation on a volcano. Interferograms also capture small changes that might be missed by other instruments.

When an eruption is predicted, the safest thing to do is to move to a another location out of the danger zone. It is also a good idea to gather emergency supplies, such as flashlights, batteries, and a radio. Long-sleeved shirts, pants, closed shoes, goggles, and a mask will also come in handy if the eruption begins before you reach safety. Staying covered will protect against burns and poisonous fumes.

It may seem like there's plenty of time to "outrun" the lava of an erupting volcano, but that's not always the case. And it's certainly not possible to run faster than rocks flying at speeds of more than 100 mph! The best way to observe nature's fiery wonder is to watch the spectacular sight from afar.

A volcanologist dresses for safety in order to collect a chunk of lava to study.

Internet Connections and Related Reading for Volcanoes

http://volcano.und.nodak.edu/vw.html
From current news to interviews with volcanologists to hundreds of questions and answers about volcanoes, this site has it all and more.

http://www.nationalgeographic.com/ngkids/0312/
Take a National Geographic journey to a mountain of fire.

http://www.fema.gov/kids/volcano.htm
The Federal Emergency Management Agency gives information about volcanoes and how to prepare for the destruction they cause.

http://www.enchantedlearning.com/subjects/volcano/
Diagrams, simple information, and activities introduce you to volcanoes.

http://science.howstuffworks.com/volcano.htm
Find out how volcanoes work at this popular science site.

* * * * * * * * * * *

Danger! Volcanoes by Seymour Simon. Simple text and photographs describe volcanoes. Chronicle Books, 2002. ISBN 1-5871-7182-1 (PB) 1-5871-7181-3 (CC). [RL 3 IL 1–3] (3424101 PB 3424102 CC)

Volcano Alert by Paul Challen. This book takes readers deep under the earth to the source of a volcano's power and then around the world to some of the most spectacular eruptions in history. Crabtree Publishing, 2004. ISBN 0-7787-1602-3 (PB) 0-7787-1570-1 (CC). [RL 3.2 IL 3–7] (3475901 PB 3475902 CC)

Volcanoes by Anna Claybourne. A first look at volcanoes. Millbrook Press, 2000. ISBN 0-7613-1173-4. [RL 3 IL 2–4] (3194806 HB)

Volcanoes by Chris Durban. Explores the birth and death of volcanoes and introduces students to plate tectonics. Blackbirch Press, 2004. ISBN 1-4103-0321-7. [RL 3 IL 1–4] (6287406 HB)

Voyage to the Volcano by Judith Stamper. The Magic School Bus takes Ms. Frizzle's class to Hawaii, where they watch a volcano blow its top. Scholastic, 2003. ISBN 0-4394-2935-8 (PB) 0-6136-3363-6 (CC). [RL 4 IL 2–4] (3414701 PB 3414702 CC)

•RL = Reading Level
•IL = Interest Level
Perfection Learning's catalog numbers are included for your ordering convenience. PB indicates paperback. CC indicates Cover Craft. HB indicates hardback.

Glossary

active
(AK tiv) still erupting occasionally or on a regular basis

cinder
(SIN der) small piece of charred wood or coal, especially one that continues to glow

cinder cone volcano
(SIN der kohn vol KAY noh) volcano with a cone-shaped top formed from volcanic material building up around the vent (see separate entry for *vent*)

crater
(KRAY ter) round, funnel-shaped depression produced by volcanic eruption

dormant
(DOR muhnt) not having erupted in a long time but still having the potential to do so

extinct
(EK stinkt) not likely to erupt again; no longer active

ground deformation
(grownd def or MAY shuhn) change in the land on or around a volcano caused by moving magma

hot spot
(haht spaht) area under the Earth's crust where magma collects

lava
(LAH vah) hot, flowing rock that reaches the Earth's surface

lava dome
(LAH vah dohm) mound of nonflowing lava that piles up near a volcano's vent (see separate entry for *vent*)

magma
(MAG muh) hot, flowing rock beneath the Earth's surface

mantle
(MAN tuhl) layer of the Earth underneath the crust where magma forms

plume
(ploom) column

pyroclastic bomb
(peye roh KLAS tik bahm)
large volcanic rock that cools
and hardens in the air

ridge
(ridj) raised area of land
resulting from magma rising
between tectonic plates and
cooling (see separate entry for
tectonic plate)

satellite
(SAT uh leyet) object put into
orbit around the Earth to collect
information and send it back to
Earth

shield volcano
(sheeld vol KAY noh) broad,
rounded volcano formed from a
buildup of lava

stratovolcano
(strat oh vol KAY noh) steep,
cone-shaped volcano created
from violently erupted cinders
and ash (see separate entry for
cinder)

summit
(SUH mit) highest point on a
mountain or volcano

tectonic plate
(tek TAHN ik playt) piece of
the Earth's crust

tephra
(TEF rah) solid material, such
as rock and ash, that explodes
out of a volcano

trench
(trench) long, narrow valley on
the ocean floor

vapor pressure
(VAY per PRESH er)
pressure exerted by a vapor, or
gas

vent
(vent) opening in the Earth's
crust from which magma
escapes

viscosity
(vis KAH sit ee) thick, sticky
consistency; ability to resist
flowing

Index